DYNAMIC DUOS OF SCIENCE

CHARLES DARWIN
AND
ALFRED RUSSEL WALLACE

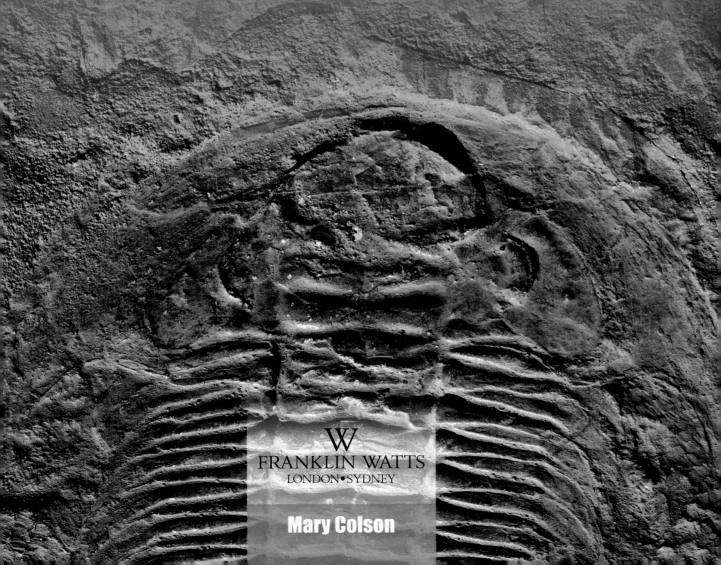

W
FRANKLIN WATTS
LONDON•SYDNEY

Mary Colson

Franklin Watts
First published in Great Britain in 2016 by The Watts Publishing Group

Credits
Produced by Calcium
Series Editors: Sarah Eason and Jennifer Sanderson
Series Designer: Keith Williams
Picture researcher: Rachel Blount

Photo credits: Cover: Library of Congress: George Grantham Bain Collection (left); Wikimedia Commons: John Gould (background), London Stereoscopic & Photographic Company (right); Inside: Dreamstime: Rodolfo Clix 36, Kelpfish 29; Shutterstock: Alex011973 45, Solodov Alexey 31b, Guido Amrein 17, Anekoho 37, Beboy 4, Ryan M. Bolton 23, Dave Coadwell 34, Paul Cowan 35, EtiAmmos 24, IrinaK 31t, Jorg Hackemann 20, JO973 18, Rosalie Kreulen 12l, 40, Piotr Krzeslak 39, Alberto Loyo 15, Mara008 42, MarcelClemens 38, MichaelTaylor3d 43, Natursports 5, 10, Paul Nicholas 13, Michal Ninger 1, 16, Olga Popova 9, Semmick Photo 11, Michelle Sole 44, Sunsinger 22, Szefei 25, Mike Taylor 33, Titelio 21, Tristan3D 41, Worldswildlifewonders 6, Oleg Znamenskiy 12r; Wikimedia Commons: Charles Darwin 27, John Gould 3, Keulemans 19, Library of Congress/Bain News Service 26, Michelangelo/Artworksforever 7, Mario Modesto 28, R. T. Pritchett 14t, Sémhur/CC-BY-SA-3.0 14b, The Hornet 32, Ben Tillman 30, Wellcome Trust 8.

Dewey number: 576.8'2'0922
ISBN: 978 1 4451 4480 1

Printed in China

Franklin Watts
An imprint of
Hachette Children's Group
Part of The Watts Publishing Group
Carmelite House
50 Victoria Embankment
London EC4Y 0DZ

An Hachette UK Company
www.hachette.co.uk

www.franklinwatts.co.uk

Contents

CHAPTER 1

The Idea That Shook the World!

Charles Darwin was born in England in 1809. He was a brilliant scientist who changed the way we think about life on Earth. His theory about the evolution of plants and animals transformed science and shocked nineteenth-century society to its core.

The nineteenth century was an age of discovery, labelling, organising and collecting. New species were being identified all the time and people marvelled at new discoveries. When Charles Darwin suggested that evolution, rather than God, had created the natural wonders of the world, people were both outraged and fascinated. Darwin's theory put him at direct odds with people of faith, including his own wife, and bishops preached against his ungodly ideas. Darwin believed that all species have to adapt to changes in their environment in order to survive. He called this 'natural selection'.

Darwin was also a leading geologist studying volcanoes, coral reefs and other Earth processes.

Both Darwin and Wallace studied the species and ecosystems of the Galápagos Islands, inlcuding this marine iguana.

The forgotten man?

Alfred Russel Wallace, a Welsh naturalist, was born in 1823. He developed a theory of natural selection at the same time as Darwin. He too collected specimens, wrote books and thought about how species might have developed in order to survive. Wallace's contribution to the theory of evolution was significant – a letter written by Wallace to Darwin changed the course of science forever.

IN THEIR OWN WORDS

To explain his theory, Darwin said:

'It is not the strongest of the species that survives, nor the most intelligent that survives. It is the one that is the most adaptable to change.'

Explaining a Duckbill Platypus

The duckbill platypus is a very strange-looking animal. Its bill is like a duck's, its feet are like an otter's and its tail is like a beaver's. The platypus is a mammal but it lays eggs and it is also venomous. When nineteenth-century zoologists saw it, they thought it must be a joke. It was not a joke, Darwin said, but the result of thousands of years of evolution.

In the early to mid-nineteenth century, many people believed that humans were descended from Adam and Eve, and that God made the world in seven days, along with all its birds and animals. People who believe this are called creationists because they believe that God created everything on Earth.

The duckbill platypus has evolved some unique features to deter predators.

The ceiling of the Sistine Chapel shows a fresco painted by Michelangelo, which depicts God and the creation of man. It was painted between 1508 and 1512. Darwin's work argued that man was created by millions of years of evolution.

Creationism and evolution

In 1859, Charles Darwin published his great work *On the Origin of Species*, and the debate between creationism and evolution began. Creationists argue that species are 'fixed' because God has created them. There is no change, natural selection or evolution. According to the Bible, the Earth is about 6,000 years old, but Darwin's theory of evolution says that it must be millions of years old because evolution takes an extremely long time.

IN THEIR OWN WORDS

In his book *On the Origin of Species*, Darwin said:

'I see no good reasons why the views given in this volume should shock the religious views of anyone.'

Passion for Nature

Darwin's fascination with nature began in his childhood. Growing up, his main influence was his grandfather, Erasmus Darwin, who was a zoologist. Wallace's interest in the natural world began later, at around the age of 18, when he was working as a land surveyor near Neath in Wales. There, he started collecting plants and learning how to label them. He would go on to gather one of the world's largest collections of plants and animals.

Wallace had a great passion for collecting. Today, his collection can be seen at the Natural History Museum in London.

Changing ideas

The study of geology was one of the big scientific developments in the nineteenth century. Naturalists, including Darwin and Wallace, read Charles Lyell's book, *The Principles of Geology*. Lyell's ideas of a gradual change in the landscape caused by volcanic eruptions and earthquakes clashed with biblical ideas, which said that disasters, such as Noah's flood, caused these changes. The new 'geological time', measured using fossils and rock layers, also clashed with the Bible's idea of how creation happened. Years later, Darwin came to know Lyell as a friend. This friendship may have been key in allowing Darwin to publish his ideas about evolution before Wallace, and ultimately claim the theory of evolution as his own.

Darwin, shown here in 1840 aged 31, ten years after he read Charles Lyell's book, The Principles of Geology. *Darwin read every new science book as it was published.*

BEHIND THE SCIENCE

Erasmus Darwin wrote a book called *Zoonomia* in 1794–1796. In it he put forward ideas about evolution, but the book was ahead of its time and Erasmus had no proof. However, his enthusiasm for the natural world sparked his grandson's interest.

A Life-Changing Letter

In 1825, Charles Darwin went to the University of Edinburgh to study medicine, like his father and elder brother before him. It was soon clear that he was not suited to a medical career because he hated the sight of blood! Then Darwin went to the University of Cambridge to study for a religious degree, which his father hoped would lead to his son becoming a vicar.

At Cambridge, Darwin read books by the great natural scientists of the day, including Alexander von Humboldt's *Personal Narrative*, which detailed his scientific travels in the Americas. These books inspired Darwin, and he planned to visit Tenerife, an island off the coast of Africa, to study its natural history. Unfortunately, money was short and Darwin went no further than Wales!

Darwin was desperate to visit Tenerife in the Canary Islands, where creatures such as this fangtooth moray eel live. He dreamed of seeing tropical scenery and vegetation.

Collectors such as Darwin and Wallace discovered the many varieties that one single species alone can exhibit.

An amazing opportunity

When he returned from his trip, a letter was waiting for Darwin. It was from one of his Cambridge friends, John Stevens Henslow, a professor of botany. This letter would not only change Darwin's life, it would also change the world. The letter was an invitation to go to sea on a naval survey ship.

BEHIND THE SCIENCE

Darwin's cousin, William Darwin Fox, was also at the University of Cambridge. Together, the cousins travelled into the fens, the flat and windy land near Cambridge, and collected butterflies, insects, beetles and moths. They identified them and even found some new species.

CHAPTER 2
Voyages of Discovery

Darwin and Wallace were about to make their own very different voyages of discovery, which would take them to places and show them species beyond their wildest dreams. They would also make discoveries and begin to draw conclusions that would continue to cause debate more than 150 years later.

The *HMS Beagle* left Plymouth on the 27th December, 1831, bound for South America. Robert FitzRoy, a naturalist, was the ship's captain. As a survey ship, the crew of the *Beagle* had to make a series of observations. These included tidal movements, ocean currents and trade winds. They also had to map coral reef islands and any natural harbours they found in South America.

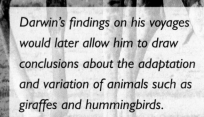

Darwin's findings on his voyages would later allow him to draw conclusions about the adaptation and variation of animals such as giraffes and hummingbirds.

Wallace wanted to be able to identify the plants growing around his home in Neath, Wales. He bought books to help him and started collecting and pressing the specimens.

Dreaming of adventures

Wallace was still at school when Darwin was on his voyage. It was when Wallace turned 18 and moved to the Neath area of Wales that his interest in natural history really took off. He worked in land surveying and began collecting specimens from the countryside. He spent his spare time reading books on natural history, including Robert Chambers' *Vestiges of the Natural History of Creation*, which suggested the theory of evolution, but did not have any proof.

IN THEIR OWN WORDS

Alfred Wallace said:

'... we became travellers, collectors and observers, in some of the richest and most interesting portions of the Earth ...'

13

All Aboard the *Beagle*!

When he left England, Darwin had no idea that he would not return for five years. The prospect of exotic travel, fantastic discoveries and a great adventure was thrilling to the young man.

Life on board the *Beagle* was a steady round of observations and recording for official reports. It was, after all, a survey ship, and its mission was to measure natural features such as tides, trade winds and coastlines. This knowledge would benefit Great Britain when it came to choosing future trading partners.

The voyage of the Beagle *took Darwin around the world.*

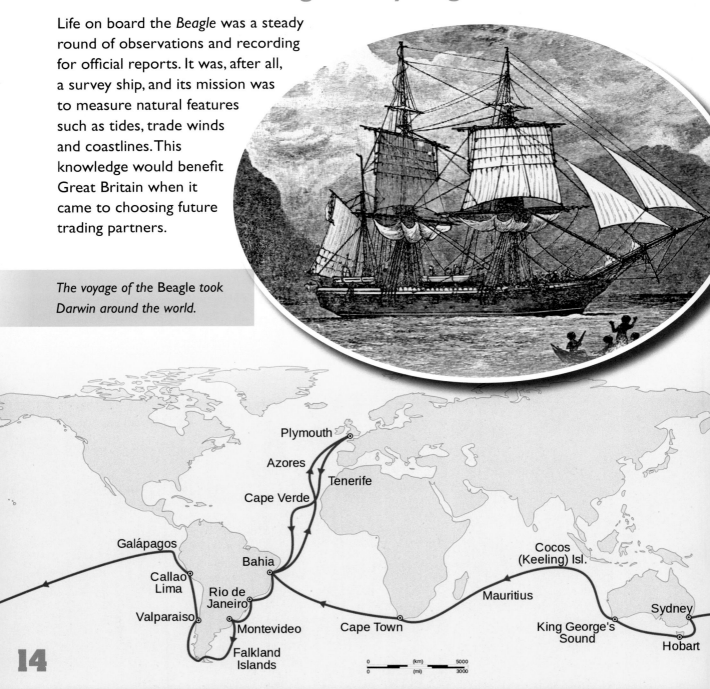

Plymouth

Azores

Tenerife

Cape Verde

Galápagos

Bahia

Callao
Lima

Rio de
Janeiro

Valparaiso

Montevideo

Falkland
Islands

Cape Town

Mauritius

Cocos
(Keeling) Isl.

King George's
Sound

Sydney

Hobart

During the voyage, Darwin puzzled over various species. Emus, for example, are flightless birds with tiny wings. Darwin wanted to know why the birds had evolved like this.

Natural variety

During the voyage, Darwin wrote notes on the landscapes of Tenerife and the Azores (islands off the coast of Africa) along with notes on marine animals. As the trip progressed, his cabin became a mini laboratory and museum, and Darwin spent many hours studying his samples. He also had plenty of time to read, think and theorise.

BEHIND THE SCIENCE

Every known species is given a unique two-part scientific name. This system, called 'binomial nomenclature', was invented in 1753, before Darwin's time. The names tell us about the plant or animal's relationship to other species. For example, the *Rhea darwinii* is a large, flightless bird native to South America. '*Rhea*' refers to a family of birds and '*darwinii*' refers to Darwin and tells us that the bird is different from other rheas. More than 120 animal species have been named after Darwin.

Coral in the Cliffs

During his voyage on the *Beagle*, Darwin read Lyell's book, *The Principles of Geology*, which set his mind racing with ideas.

When the *Beagle* stopped at the remote island of St. Jago in the Cape Verde Islands, off the coast of Africa, Darwin thought that the island's volcanic landscape was rather lifeless. However, as he began to explore, he found fertile valleys teeming with life. On St. Jago, Darwin also saw rock formations that suggested Lyell's theory about Earth's geological history was correct.

On his journey, Darwin found a species of isopod that reminded him of trilobite fossils. Trilobites were arthropods that lived over 250 million years ago.

These cliffs in Cape Verde once formed the sea floor. Darwin realised this when he found coral fossils within the rock.

Theory and observation

Up in the cliffs, high above sea level, Darwin saw coral fossils. By looking at these, he could see that different species had lived on Earth at different times. He could also see that, over time, some species had become extinct and new ones had taken their place. As the *Beagle* sailed on, Darwin became obsessed with two questions: how did this change happen and why did it happen?

BEHIND THE SCIENCE

In the eighteenth century, the geologist James Hutton had presented a theory about the changing nature of Earth's crust. Later, Charles Lyell developed Hutton's ideas. Both men said that slow-moving forces acting over a very long period of time shaped the crust. Lyell was one of the first scientists to believe that the world was older than 300 million years. His ideas were shocking to ordinary people and many scientists.

Wallace in South America

Wallace had been inspired to travel, explore and collect after reading Darwin's own account of his journey, *The Voyage of The Beagle*. In 1848, 17 years after Darwin had set off on the *Beagle*, Wallace left England, bound for Brazil.

Wallace's friend, Henry Bates, was with him on board the *Mischief*. Bates was an entomologist: an insect expert. Bates and Wallace's plan was to collect insects and animal specimens and sell them to collectors in England. Wallace and Bates collected specimens near the port town of Belém do Pará on the River Amazon. Wallace also explored the rainforest in the Rio Negro region. His mind whirred with excitement as he observed the natural wonders before his eyes.

The toucan is native to Central and South America. Wallace wondered why the toucan was not found elsewhere.

Wallace drew this image of a tree frog that he saw in South America.

Disaster at sea

During Wallace's voyage home, a fire forced the crew to abandon its ship. All of the specimens Wallace had collected were lost. He could save only part of his diary and a few sketches. After his return, despite having lost most of his notes and diaries from his South American expedition, Wallace wrote many academic papers and books detailing his findings. He also started to make connections with other naturalists, including Darwin.

IN THEIR OWN WORDS

About the natural beauty he saw, Wallace said:

'It is here, too, that the rarest birds, the most lovely insects and the most interesting mammals and reptiles are to be found.'

CHAPTER 3

Questions and Answers

The mid-nineteenth century was buzzing with scientific developments and major discoveries. It was a confident time because much of the world had been explored and there was a feeling that everything that there was to know about Earth was already known.

The study of zoology and natural science was enjoying a boom. In the 1850s, the first complete dinosaur skeletons were found in North America. Prior to this time, only partial skeletons had been unearthed. Darwin and Wallace were just two of many scientists who were travelling further and exploring deeper into the natural world than ever before. What they found was extraordinary.

The discovery of dinosaur skeletons in the nineteenth century raised questions about why these creatures became extinct. This T. rex fossil is on display at the American Museum of Natural History in New York.

Collecting evidence

The questions being asked by Darwin and Wallace challenged previous theories. They looked for answers by collecting, observing and making hundreds of pages of detailed notes. On his voyage, Darwin had preserved samples of insects in alcohol. Larger animals were stuffed. He left the specimens boxed up in port ready to be shipped back to Great Britain. He planned to study them when he arrived home, believing that they could contain the answers he was looking for.

Using a microscope such as the one show here allowed Darwin and Wallace to note tiny differences between species.

IN THEIR OWN WORDS

When Darwin arrived back home after his voyage on the *Beagle*, he said:

'My head is quite confused with so much delight.'

Darwin in the Galápagos Islands

The *Beagle* sailed all around South America, along the coast of Argentina, around Tierra del Fuego and up the coast of Chile. Darwin thought he had already seen all the wonders the continent could reveal when the ship arrived at what he could only describe as 'paradise' – the Galápagos Islands.

The Galápagos are a group of volcanic islands in the Pacific Ocean. They are one of the least polluted places on Earth, and are so remote that only a few people have ever been there. With very few natural predators, the islands are home to a wide variety of some of the most amazing animals on Earth.

The spectacular and remote Galápagos Islands are a paradise for wildlife. They are home to hundreds of species that are unique to the islands.

Variation of species

Darwin noticed that species varied even between islands that were close to each other and that also had similar landscapes. Giant tortoises on different islands, for example, were a different size and had a different neck length and shell shape. Darwin wondered what had caused this variation within species.

There are 14 subspecies of giant tortoise living on different Galápagos islands.

BEHIND THE SCIENCE

In a population of living things, some are better able to survive than others. For example, an animal that can run fast away from predators is likely to live longer than one that is less fast. An animal that lives longer is likely to produce more offspring. In so doing, it passes its running ability to its offspring. So in the next generation, there will be more animals better able to survive. Darwin named this process natural selection, or 'survival of the fittest'. It means that animals with a variation that helps them survive in an environment gradually dominate the population.

23

Wallace's Malay Adventure

In 1854, less than two years after his return from Brazil, Wallace set off again. This time, his destinations were Singapore, Malaysia and Indonesia. Wallace spent nearly eight years in the regions, visiting every major island. He studied, collected, sampled and preserved with an amazing passion.

When Wallace returned, he had collected almost 110,000 insects, 7,500 shells, 8,050 bird skins and 410 mammal and reptile specimens. He also discovered several thousand species that were new to science. On Bacan Island, he named Wallace's Golden Birdwing Butterfly. He also discovered Wallace's Standard-Wing Bird of Paradise.

The beautiful Wallace's Golden Birdwing Butterfly is just one of dozens of species that Wallace discovered.

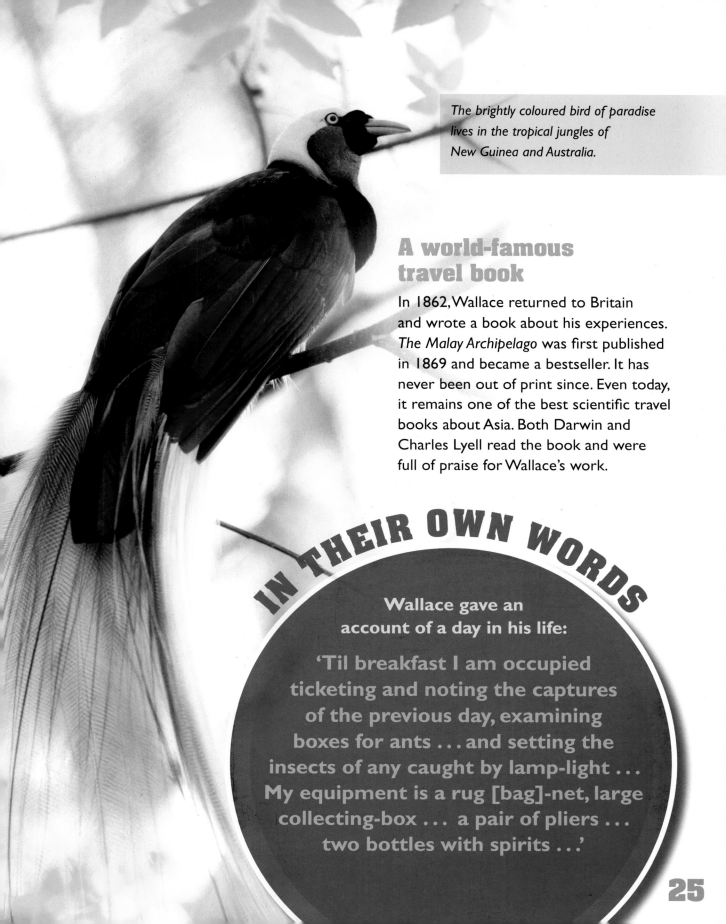

The brightly coloured bird of paradise lives in the tropical jungles of New Guinea and Australia.

A world-famous travel book

In 1862, Wallace returned to Britain and wrote a book about his experiences. *The Malay Archipelago* was first published in 1869 and became a bestseller. It has never been out of print since. Even today, it remains one of the best scientific travel books about Asia. Both Darwin and Charles Lyell read the book and were full of praise for Wallace's work.

IN THEIR OWN WORDS

Wallace gave an account of a day in his life:

'Til breakfast I am occupied ticketing and noting the captures of the previous day, examining boxes for ants ... and setting the insects of any caught by lamp-light ... My equipment is a rug [bag]-net, large collecting-box ... a pair of pliers ... two bottles with spirits ...'

CHAPTER 4

The Race for Proof

The idea of evolution had been around for a long time, but it was Darwin and Wallace who struck upon the theory of evolution by natural selection. They proposed that new species evolve as nature selects the variation in characteristics that best help a living thing surive. By the mid-1850s, the race to be the first to prove the theory. Darwin was in poor health while Wallace was exploring the jungles of Borneo, gathering new evidence.

Darwin believed that all species share a common pair of parent ancestors. He studied pigeons to show how one parent pair could produce stronger offspring. He bred pigeons with different colours and of different sizes to see which parent birds produced the strongest offspring. Darwin called this selective breeding or unnatural selection. His investigations meant that farmers could make new, stronger animal breeds in just a few generations.

Darwin had been working on his theory of evolution for more than 20 years – it had absorbed almost all of his time and energies.

Alarm bells!

In 1855, Wallace wrote a paper on evolution called *Sarawak Law,* which Charles Lyell read. When Lyell went to visit Darwin, Darwin excitedly told him about his great theory of evolution. No doubt thinking of Wallace's progress on the subject, Lyell urged Darwin to publish his theory as soon as he possibly could.

Darwin's sketch shows how evolution and variation between species occurred.

BEHIND THE SCIENCE

Unnatural selection is the basis for modern genetic research and for the genetic engineering of animals and plants. All living things are determined by their genes, the code for life. Scientists can now alter or change genes to make species stronger or more productive.

A Letter from Wallace

With Lyell's encouragement, Darwin began to work on an outline of his theory. Meanwhile, Wallace was working on his own development of *Sarawak Law*. In 1855, Darwin received a letter from Wallace, which showed that he was close to making his theories about natural selection public, before Darwin had a chance to publish his own ideas. Wallace had written a paper called *On the Tendency of Varieties to Depart Indefinitely from the Original Type*. This discussed the huge variety to be found in species and how they adapt and change. It was the basis for the theory of natural selection.

Darwin felt as though his whole life's work was in the balance. If he could not focus his mind and complete the write up of his great idea, then Wallace was going to win all the glory. Darwin had been sickly and his health could barely stand the stress and the strain. On top of his physical symptoms, he started to have severe panic attacks, which left him depressed and unable to work.

Darwin's home, Down House, was where he carried out his most important work. He and his family lived here for more than 40 years.

Joint winners?

In July 1858, Charles Lyell and Thomas Hooker presented Darwin's theory of evolution and proof at a meeting of the famous Linnean Society of London. They also presented the letter that Wallace had sent to Darwin. In the society's journal of August that year, Darwin's contributions were placed before Wallace's essay, which showed that it was Darwin who had first discovered natural selection.

By studying barnacles, one of the least understood life forms, Darwin could finally prove his theory of evolution. Darwin believed that if he could classify these complex life forms and explain how they had evolved it would add credibility to and help prove his theory.

IN THEIR OWN WORDS

Darwin said:

'It is a cursed evil to any man to become as absorbed in any subject as I am in mine.'

Darwin's Masterpiece

In 1859, Charles Darwin's book on evolution and natural selection was published. Its full title is *On the Origin of Species by Means of Natural Selection, or the Preservation of Favoured Races in the Struggle for Life*. Darwin's theory challenged all previous ideas about creation and the book changed the natural science landscape forever.

Darwin's fragile health was unsettled with all the worry about what society would think of him. At one point prior to publication, he told his wife to publish the book after his death. He said to one friend that publishing the book was like 'confessing to a murder'. He told another that he was 'living in Hell'. He even started to refer to his great work as his 'abominable volume'. However, he was certain that his theory was correct.

On the Origin of Species *was one of the most revolutionary books ever written and it is still in print.*

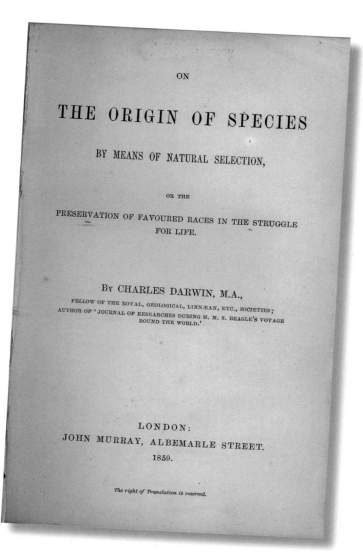

ON

THE ORIGIN OF SPECIES

BY MEANS OF NATURAL SELECTION,

OR THE

PRESERVATION OF FAVOURED RACES IN THE STRUGGLE FOR LIFE.

BY CHARLES DARWIN, M.A.,
FELLOW OF THE ROYAL, GEOLOGICAL, LINNÆAN, ETC., SOCIETIES;
AUTHOR OF 'JOURNAL OF RESEARCHES DURING H. M. S. BEAGLE'S VOYAGE
ROUND THE WORLD.'

LONDON:
JOHN MURRAY, ALBEMARLE STREET.
1859.

The right of Translation is reserved.

Road to recovery

Just before his book was published, Darwin became very ill again and went to the spa town of Ilkley in Yorkshire to take a water cure. He stayed there for nine weeks. As he recovered far away from London, he was on the verge of becoming one of the most famous and controversial figures of all time.

Darwin saw the armadillo in South America. He was determined to discover why a creature had evolved in such a strange way.

IN THEIR OWN WORDS

In *On the Origin of Species* Darwin explained natural selection:

'I think it inevitably follows, that as new species in the course of time are formed through natural selection, others will become rarer and rarer, and finally extinct. The forms which stand in closest competition with those undergoing modification and improvement will naturally suffer most.'

There are no natural predators of the Kakapo of New Zealand. Therefore, the species has never developed wings strong enough for flight.

CHAPTER 5
Heroes and Villains

The national and international reaction to his book was beyond anything Darwin could have prepared himself for. Everyone had a say on the new theory, from botanists and the British prime minister to bishops and people on railway station platforms. The book was hugely popular, scandalising, fascinating and controversial in almost equal measure.

Charles Kingsley, a Christian novelist, wrote to Darwin praising his work. He said: 'If you be right I must give up much that I have believed.' Many people were horrified that Darwin had taken God out of creation. They believed that new species were evidence of God's work. People also struggled to accept Darwin's proposal that humans were just another animal and had evolved too. Academics, people of faith and those without faith argued the finer points of evolution versus creation. It is a debate that still continues even today.

Darwin and his theory were mocked in many newspaper cartoons.

Today, Darwin is considered one of Britain's scientific heroes and his image is printed on the British £10 note.

Darwin's supporters

Alfred Wallace returned to Britain in 1862 and became one of Darwin's most energetic defenders. He would later even write a book in defence of the theory called *Darwinism: An Exposition of the Theory of Natural Selection, with Some of Its Applications*. Darwin's friends, Charles Lyell and the biologist Thomas Huxley, also supported his theory.

IN THEIR OWN WORDS

In defence of his theory, Darwin said:

'We can allow satellites, planets, suns, universe, nay whole systems of universe, to be governed by laws, but the smallest insect, we wish to be created at once by special act.'

The Great Showdown

The debate about evolution and its merits rolled on. The tug of war between those of faith, those of science and the millions in between kept Darwin and his theory in the spotlight. The great debate between evolution and creationism reached its climax on the 30th June, 1860, in Oxford, where the two sides met to argue their cases.

Darwin himself was too ill to attend the debate. The criticism and backlash against both him and his theory had taken its toll on his health. Instead, his friend Thomas Huxley took his place. On the other side stood the powerful and influential figure of the Bishop of Oxford, Samuel Wilberforce.

This statue of Thomas Huxley – 'Darwin's bulldog' – is on display at the Natural History Museum in London.

Thomas H
philosopher
most influen
His work on co
him acclaim as
defence of the
him notoriety as

Huxley was a gr
and people flocke
He wrote science
on education were
colleges throughout Brit

The Natural History Museum in Oxford houses an amazing collection of dinosaur fossils, extinct species and man-made curiosities.

Man or monkey?

It was not long before strong emotions and insults rose to the surface. At one point, Wilberforce is said to have asked Huxley about humans descending from monkeys and whether he himself was a monkey. The audience laughed. Huxley replied that 'he would much rather have a monkey for his grandfather than a man who could indulge in jokes on such a subject'.

BEHIND THE SCIENCE

The Oxford Museum of Natural History was built to house the University of Oxford's collections of natural history specimens and man-made objects. The two collections were housed in separate areas. The professors believed this was important to separate human achievement from the wonder of God and creation.

Darwin's Final Years

After publishing *On the Origin of Species*, Darwin settled back into his research. His mind kept returning to an idea proposed by the economist Thomas Malthus. Malthus had written that when human populations cannot produce enough food, the weakest starve, die of disease or are killed in fighting – only the strong survive. Darwin thought that the same could apply to animals, and that those with useful characteristics survived and passed these on to their young.

In the nineteenth century, most people believed that there was a natural hierarchy in nature and that humans had a far higher status than any other creature. From his earlier work, Darwin did not believe this and was convinced that chimpanzees were the closest relatives of human beings.

Darwin thought there must be a connection between humans and primates, partly because their skeletons are so similar.

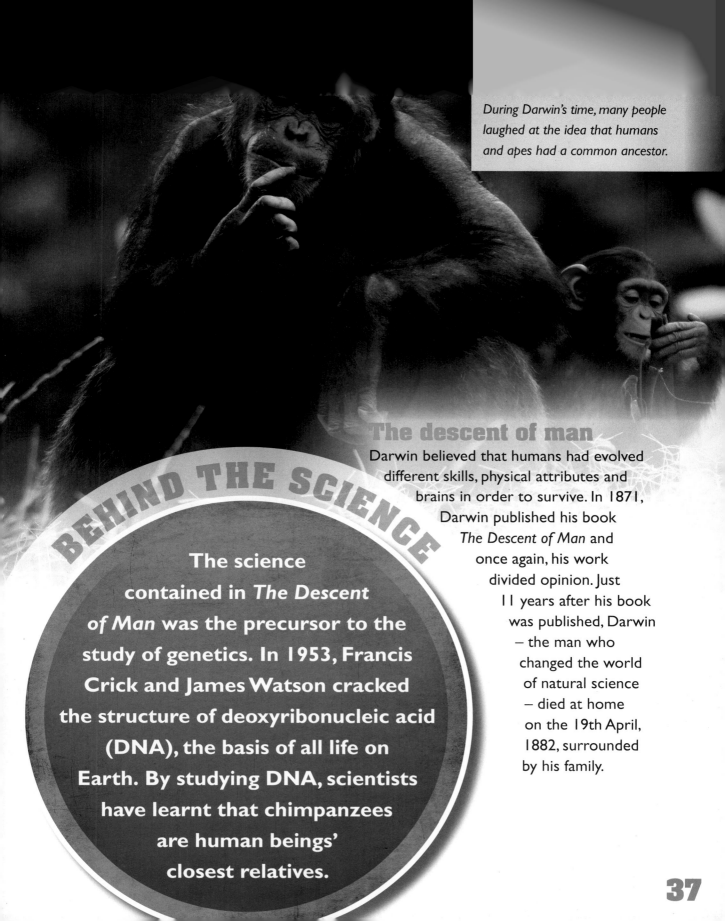

During Darwin's time, many people laughed at the idea that humans and apes had a common ancestor.

The descent of man

Darwin believed that humans had evolved different skills, physical attributes and brains in order to survive. In 1871, Darwin published his book *The Descent of Man* and once again, his work divided opinion. Just 11 years after his book was published, Darwin – the man who changed the world of natural science – died at home on the 19th April, 1882, surrounded by his family.

BEHIND THE SCIENCE

The science contained in *The Descent of Man* was the precursor to the study of genetics. In 1953, Francis Crick and James Watson cracked the structure of deoxyribonucleic acid (DNA), the basis of all life on Earth. By studying DNA, scientists have learnt that chimpanzees are human beings' closest relatives.

CHAPTER 6

Life After Evolution

During his life, Darwin had convinced many scientists that evolution and natural selection were correct. In June 1909, scientists from all over the world gathered in Cambridge to commemorate the fiftieth anniversary of *On the Origin of Species*. Today, each year on the 12th February, Darwin Day is celebrated all over the world.

However, since Darwin's death, the debate between creationism and evolution has continued. In some countries, some schools still teach creationism, calling it 'intelligent design'.

Scientists and some people of faith still differ in their opinion about how Earth came into existence.

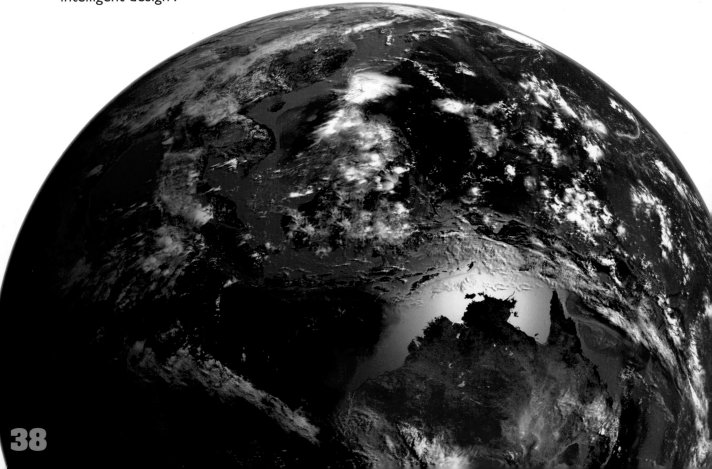

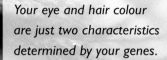
Your eye and hair colour are just two characteristics determined by your genes.

The Scopes Monkey Trial

By the early 1920s, it had become illegal to teach children about evolution in parts of the United States. *The Butler Act* was a law that stated that only creationism could be taught in Tennessee. In 1925, John T. Scopes was put on trial for teaching evolution. The whole country was hooked and eager to witness the outcome. Scopes was found guilty and fined.

Over the past 100 years, biologists have accepted Darwin's theory of natural selection. Modern biologists, such as Richard Dawkins, are developing Darwin's ideas and building on them in their own research on genetics.

BEHIND THE SCIENCE

Every cell of the human body contains chromosomes. Humans have 46 chromosomes and each one is made of a long material called **DNA**. A gene is a short section of **DNA**. Genes determine our bodies' characteristics. For example, a gene, or a combination of genes, determines eye colour. Genes are passed from parents to offspring.

The Most Famous Man in the World?

After Charles Darwin died, Alfred Russel Wallace continued his studies and research into the natural world and evolution. By the turn of the century, he was probably one of the most famous men in the world. His extraordinary contribution to natural science includes hundreds of academic papers and more than 20 books.

Although today Wallace is often considered the forgotten man of evolution, his part in bringing the theory of natural selection to wider acceptance was vital. He kept his enthusiasm and interest for natural history to the very end of his life. Wallace's great talent was in explaining the complexities of evolution and natural history in everyday terms. People flocked to his lectures to hear the great man speak.

Wallace mapped the locations of over 20,000 vertebrates, including tree frogs such as this one.

There is even a crater on Mars named after Wallace!

Honours and achievements

In 1870, Wallace was elected president of the Entomological Society of London. A few years later, he was awarded the Order of Merit, the highest honour that can be given to a British citizen. He also received awards from academic institutions overseas. In 1893, he was elected to the Royal Society and in 1908, he was awarded the Linnean Society's new Darwin-Wallace Medal. Soon after this, in 1913, he died in Dorset.

IN THEIR OWN WORDS

Wallace said:

'In all works on natural history, we constantly find details of the marvellous adaptation of animals to their food, their habits and the localities in which they are found.'

41

Darwin, Wallace and Modern Science

The important work of Charles Darwin and Alfred Wallace lives on in the work of scientists today, but where have their theories led us and how have they furthered science?

The Human Genome Project is the world's largest biology project and will eventually tell us which genes cause what effect, from eye colour to heart and brain function. Gene research has already had one major success. Scientists are able to isolate the genes that cause some inherited diseases. This means that they can treat them earlier, learn more about the diseases and make more effective medicines.

Today we understand that DNA is the chemical building block of all life. Darwin and Wallace's exploration of the natural world and the evolution of life on Earth paved the way for later scientists to further explore and understand the genetic make-up of animal and plant bodies.

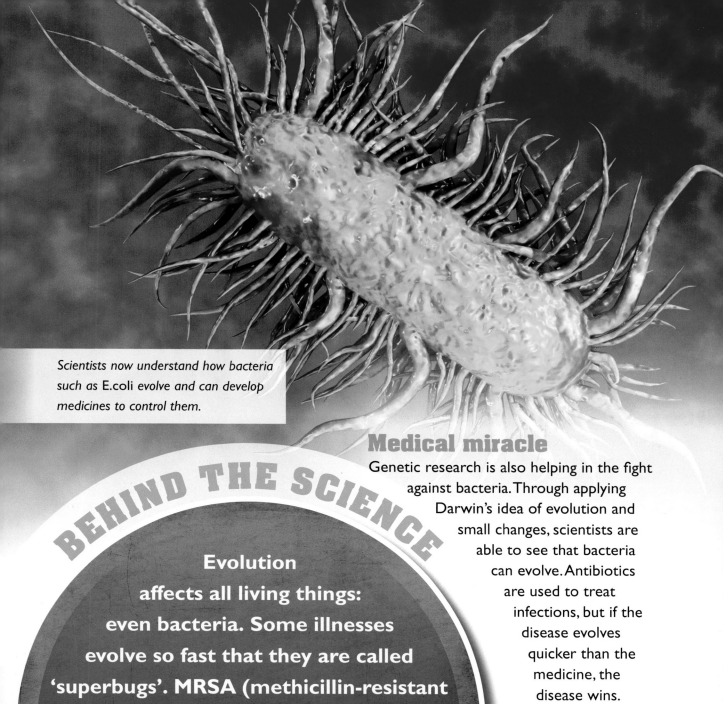

Scientists now understand how bacteria such as E.coli evolve and can develop medicines to control them.

Medical miracle

Genetic research is also helping in the fight against bacteria. Through applying Darwin's idea of evolution and small changes, scientists are able to see that bacteria can evolve. Antibiotics are used to treat infections, but if the disease evolves quicker than the medicine, the disease wins.

By studying the rate of evolution, scientists are able to keep ahead of the bacteria. This helps to save millions of lives every year.

BEHIND THE SCIENCE

Evolution affects all living things: even bacteria. Some illnesses evolve so fast that they are called 'superbugs'. MRSA (methicillin-resistant *Staphylococcus aureus*) is a bacteria that evolves quickly. Sometimes superbugs can be treated with antibiotics, but they change how they attack the body so fast that the medicine cannot keep up.

The Debate Continues

Darwin and Wallace changed the way we approach the study of natural history and challenged the idea of a creator. Darwin, in particular, became a target for criticism and even hatred. Today, we know that the theory of evolution by natural selection is how life on Earth has developed. Their work has had a lasting impact on both science and society. It has led to modern genetic studies and it has encouraged greater understanding and appreciation of the wonders of the natural world.

Prior to Darwin's book, the work of scientists was to find out what was behind nature to explain how God worked. Darwin and Wallace showed that finding out about the natural world was useful for our own knowledge and for our own benefit. The modern conservation movement has its roots in Darwinism.

Many animals are now protected by conservation laws thanks to Darwin's work.

Today's scientists have continued the work begun by Darwin and Wallace.

Lasting effect

Darwin and Wallace helped us to learn about the fragile balance between humans and the environment. Through their passion for their work and their ability to communicate their theories, their work has been continued by the next generation of scientists. When Darwin was at Edinburgh University, one of his professors told him to 'study tiny detail but ask big questions'. Charles Darwin did just that and natural science and wider society have not been the same since.

IN THEIR OWN WORDS

Darwin said:

'A man who dares to waste one hour of time has not discovered the value of life.'

Glossary

botany the study of plants

controversial causing strong disagreement

deoxyribonucleic acid (DNA) the material inside cells that carries the information about how an individual will look and function. Short sections of DNA, called genes, carry each piece of information.

economist a person who studies the economy

evolution the process by which species change and develop gradually over thousands and millions of years

family a small group of living things who have similar features

gene a basic unit that can pass on characteristics from parent to offspring

genetic engineering changing or adapting genes

genus group containing animal or plant species with similar characteristics

geology the study of Earth's processes

graduation the completion of a degree course at college or university

hierarchy an order or system that has different ranks of power

inherited received from a parent

kingdom one of several large groups, such as animals or plants, to which living things on Earth belong

Linnean Society the world's oldest biological society, based in London

naturalist a person who studies the natural world

natural selection the process in which the living things that adapt to their environment and survive are more likely to produce offspring and pass their characteristics on to the next generation

Noah's flood biblical tale about a man who built a ship and saved his family and a pair of every type of animal from a great flood

primate apes, monkeys and humans

Royal Society the oldest science society in the world

species a group of animals or plants that look like each other and can interbreed

status a position in society, high or low

theorise to put forward a new idea

trade winds tropical wind that commonly blows toward the equator

venomous poisonous

vicar a priest or minister in the Church of England

water cure a treatment for illness using pure mineral water

zoologist a person who studies animals

For More Information

Books

Charles Darwin (Giants of Science), Kathleen Krull, Puffin Books

Evolve or Die (Horrible Science), Phil Gates, Scholastic

Evolution, Daniel Loxton, Kids Can Press

Evolution Revolution, Robert Winston, Dorling Kindersley

Websites

Are you cleverer than a plant? Find out at the interactive learning zone of the Darwin Trust at:
www.charlesdarwintrust.org

Find out more about Darwin and evolution at this University of Cambridge website:
darwin200.christs.cam.ac.uk/pages/index.php?page_id=j

Visit the Natural History Museum in London online to learn all about evolution and the evidence behind the theory at:
www.nhm.ac.uk/nature-online/evolution

Note to parents and teachers
Every effort has been made by the Publisher to ensure that these websites contain no inappropriate or offensive material. However, because of the nature of the Internet, it is impossible to guarantee that the contents of these sites will not be altered. We strongly advise that Internet access is supervised by a responsible adult.

Index